The Portage Poetry Series

I0528853

Series Titles

The Trouble with Being a Childless Only Child
Michelle Meyer

Happy Everything
Caitlin Cowan

Dear Lo
Brady Bove

Sadness of the Apex Predator
Dion O'Reilly

Don't Feed the Animal
Hikari Miya

Glitter City.
Bonnie Jill Emanuel

Listening to Mars
Sally Ashton

The Watching Sky
Judy Brackett Crowe

Let It Be Told in a Single Breath
Russell Thorburn

The Blue Divide
Linda Nemec Foster

Lake, River, Mountain
Mark B. Hamilton

Talking Diamonds
Linda Nemec Foster

Poetic People Power
Tara Bracco (ed.)

The Found Object Imagines a Life: New and Selected Poems
Mary Catherine Harper

Naming the Ghost
Emily Hockaday

Mourning
Dokubo Melford Goodhead

Messengers of the Gods: New and Selected Poems
Kathryn Gahl

After the 8-Ball
Colleen Alles

Careful Cartography
Devon Bohm

Broken On the Wheel
Barbara Costas-Biggs

Sparks and Disperses
Cathleen Cohen

Holding My Selves Together: New and Selected Poems
Margaret Rozga

Lost and Found Departments
Heather Dubrow

Marginal Notes
Alfonso Brezmes

The Almost-Children
Cassondra Windwalker

Meditations of a Beast
Kristine Ong Muslim

Praise for

The Trouble with Being a Childless Only Child

"Haunted, plaintive, and often darkly afflicted, the deeply felt poems of Michelle Meyer's *The Trouble with Being a Childless Only Child* rise from a great depth of human emotion—clear, forceful poems that are searingly personal. This is a book about breakage, about betrayal, about grief and loss. Ultimately, it's a richly rewarding book, one about healing and redemption, a book sutured with forgiveness and bound in love."

—Robert Hedin
author of *At the Great Door of Mourning*

"Michelle Meyer takes many issues of family head-on and offers up some deeply emotional and powerful poems. Her relationship to her mother is at the heart of this moving collection as she considers her life with her and without her. There is no poor-me here, rather a loving and clear look at what she was given and what she's done with it. While there is grief in this collection, there is a clarity and acceptance in words that are wise and earned. I loved reading these poems and know I will return to them again and again."

—Mary Logue
author of *Heart Wood: Poems*

"Michelle Meyer writes about grief with honesty, generosity, and the kind of stripped-down beauty that makes you stop and catch your breath. By turns delicate, brutal, bitterly funny, and haunting, these poems capture the evolving ways that loss and love intertwine."

—Jacqueline West
author of *Candle and Pins*

"When Michelle Meyer said she didn't like dog-eared pages, I took it as a dare and won—she has so many. I wondered how she could run the title's theme over a whole manuscript, and watched her do it—she sings and sings for her mother and finds herself in the process. These poems are painful dirges and celebratory wakes and, best of all, sometimes both at once. This book is so good, with such mature vision and no-nonsense voice, I want to see her next book right now."

—John Graber
author of *Thanksgiving Dawn: Poems 1970-2008*

"Writing about love, loss, and grief is very easy to do poorly. For Michelle Meyer to do it so effectively and effortlessly in these poems is a testament to her brilliance as a writer. She brings moments of her mother and her own story to life again, all the while ignited by the very real and tangible fear of a life being forgotten. On the contrary, what Michelle has done is crafted a portrait through these poems that has been immortalized here, impossible for any reader to forget."

—Emma Snyder
co-founder & editor-in-chief of *Tabula Rasa Review*

The Trouble
With Being
A Childless
Only Child

poems

Michelle Meyer

CORNERSTONE PRESS
UNIVERSITY OF WISCONSIN-STEVENS POINT

Cornerstone Press, Stevens Point, Wisconsin 54481
Copyright © 2024 Michelle Meyer
www.uwsp.edu/cornerstone

Printed in the United States of America by
Point Print and Design Studio, Stevens Point, Wisconsin

Library of Congress Control Number: 2023950492
ISBN: 978-1-960329-28-8

Cornerstone Press titles are produced in courses and internships offered by the
Department of English at the University of Wisconsin–Stevens Point.

DIRECTOR & PUBLISHER
Dr. Ross K. Tangedal

EXECUTIVE EDITORS
Jeff Snowbarger, Freesia McKee

EDITORIAL DIRECTOR
Ellie Atkinson

SENIOR EDITORS
Brett Hill, Grace Dahl

PRESS STAFF
Carolyn Czerwinski, Sophie McPherson, Kylie Newton, Natalie Reiter,
Alexander Soukup, Ava Willett, Cam Williams

For my mother
"The one and only"

CONTENTS

INTRODUCTION

Dear Reader,

The Trouble with Being a Childless Only Child is a manuscript I never intended to write. It was never a thought bubble or even a "good idea" that turned into a forgotten note in one of my many journals. Then, on September 18, 2019, at 12:33pm, my mother died. Her death was sudden, completely unexpected, and the trauma of it nearly broke me.

For the first two weeks afterwards, I could barely eat. The only time I held a pen was to sign my name to various documents. I could not put my grief to paper because how could I think of her in the third person? She was just here. I had just kissed her cheek and held her hand. We had just giggled over old photos together.

I felt wild with confusion and my body grew thin. A poisonous well of sorrow was swallowing me. Yes, that well contained loss, but guilt, shame, and deep regret were also mixed into the thick, oily prism.

I am my mother's only child and because I do not have a sibling with whom to share memories, laugh, or grieve with, I was terrified, almost obsessed with the possibility that I might forget not just my childhood, but everything about my mother—her eye-watering laugh, her hip swing, the way she pursed her lips, stomped her foot, flicked a fingernail, swallowed a pill by throwing her head back—even, if not especially, the many tragedies that defined her life.

In typical only-child fashion, I wanted to keep all of it, to hoard every memory that my own aging brain could recall. There was no other choice—I had to pick up a pen. The words that turned into poems came slowly, then feverishly. Once I started, I couldn't stop. I had to write. I had to document, grieve, apologize, forgive, cope, and most importantly, I had to—needed to—remember. I'll never remember everything, but these poems ensure the preservation of some things.

Thank you for opening these pages and allowing this only child an opportunity to share. Thank you for standing next to me at the well. In love and grief, I'm with you.

—Michelle Meyer

Hypothesis

Perhaps the reason my mother and her sister
opened their mouths so pelican-wide when they
each found a moment to let go and really, really
      laugh
is because as babies they'd both learned the art of
unhinging their jaws by
      enduring
their father's gut punches and face slaps.

      Therefore

by the time they learned the art of
      laughter
neither knew how to release
      pleasure
unless it felt like
      pain.

Birds, Suddenly

Driving with my maps app lit up
I noticed the blue of the sky, the heat
of the day, the wide-open road leading me
toward your closed-door emergency.
I noticed my grip
on the steering wheel, the song
on the radio being sung by Karen Carpenter
who didn't eat,
but for different reasons than the reasons
you didn't eat. Karen Carpenter,
whose heart was weak with pain
but for different reasons
than the reasons your heart was weak
with pain.
Karen Carpenter who (like you) lived a life
of emergency but (like you) still wondered
why, why, why, why, why
do birds suddenly appear?
Karen Carpenter, whose words I couldn't
expel from my head
when I saw the emergency tube
that was hiss-pumping emergency
oxygen into your lungs,
whose words I whisper-sang into your ear
over and over and over
for the same reason Karen Carpenter sang them,
for the same reason
everyone sings them—because
love.
Desperate love.

It Takes You by Surprise

Surprise birthday party.
Surprise bouquet of flowers.
Surprise visit from Ed McMahon
who hands over a surprise

two-million-dollar check.
My idea of surprise is good.
Is welcome.

I never thought about being telephoned by
The Big Bad Wolf.
That would also be surprising.

Because it's not like you expect such things.
You expect things like breakfast,
coffee, a commute.

Not things like
The Big Bad Wolf.
Not things like

an early morning phone call
from an unknown number
that slips into voicemail,

preserving forever a message from
The Big Bad Wolf
who is disguised in a white coat,

who is licking his lips and muttering
sorry-for-your-loss condolences
while leisurely sucking
the marrow from your bones.

When I Was Six I Learned About Death

I was told that it happened
when your eyes were closed.

Open your eyes, I panicked, poking
at my mother's tired feet, gripping
her smooth, warm hands because
what if? what if?

When I was 49, I learned about death.
It happened when her eyes were closed.

Open your eyes, I begged, rubbing
her pale feet—holding on
holding on, holding on,
then

letting go

of her

of her smooth, cold hands

because

Those Hips

No one could dance like my mother.
Those hips swayed
so elegantly, so wildly

that if Elvis had seen those hips move
he might have—I mean *really* might have
blushed.

Those hips
were award-winners.

Those hips scored
drinks and dates and the approval
of man after man after man—stirred

the desire of
man after man after man—raised
the eyebrow, the heartbeat, the blood pressure,

the glass, the pecker, the voice, the fist
of man after man after man.

Those hips.

WWJD

I'm not talking about Jesus. I never really knew him.
I mean—Him.
I'm talking about Judy—daughter, sister, friend, artist, woman,
wife X 3, mother X 1.

My mother

who I never fully understood but knew well enough to know that
if you brought her a beer she'd say—It's so nice
to have someone bring me a beer. She'd say—
My cat never brings me beer, and

if she was stung by a friend & the friend quoted Buddha & Buddha said,
If you're stung by a wasp, will you stop smelling the flowers?
she'd say—No, but I'd find a different patch of flowers.
Or she'd say—

Buddha?
I never really liked the guy. Or, depending on her mood,
she'd say—
Yes—All flowers be damned!

But probably she'd breathe a heavy sigh and say—Well, WWJD?
Only she'd be talking about Jesus,
because even though she never really knew Him and
even though (for the record) He never once brought her a beer,
He's still the only man she ever really trusted.

24 Hours Before the Emergency

I went to bed thinking,
I can't do this. I can't Care all the time.

I woke up thinking,
clean the house, get ready to Care.

There was a message.
Call—it's an emergency. Call—I'm dying.

Call. Come. Care.

Give me a minute.
Give me an hour. I need to run. I just need

to run before I—
Call. Come. Care.

Before the last time that I will ever—
Call. Come. Care.

I can't do this.
I want to run.

Groceries for Mom

Rice Krispies
that she'll never eat

Sliced turkey
White bread
that she'll never eat

Fish
Mashed potatoes
Cooked carrots

that she'll never eat

Jello
that she'll never eat

Sugar Cookies
that she always loved
that she'll never eat
that I'll serve at her memorial
along with the coffee and the

Peanut Butter Cookies
that she also loved
that she'll never eat
that I'll never eat
that a man I've never seen before
that she'll never see again
will mindlessly munch on

as he leans in to get a closer look
at an old picture of her
sexy legs, perky breasts, and full lips,
crumbs spilling from his mouth and
littering a floor that he'll
never sweep

Limbo

I had never been aware of how often I peed
until peeing meant
leaving
the room where my mother lay
dying.

Steely ICU doors opened before me, a remote
controlled passageway between life and—

Turn right, walk down the Grand Hall.
Turn left.
The Ladies Room is just before the
Waiting Room. The
Waiting-For-Everything-To-Change Room.

The Limbo Room. The Purgatory Room. The In-Between Room
where at 2:30 a.m. all the chairs and couches covered
in outdated geometric fabrics
sit empty
except for one recliner that's filled by a fat man snoring
in front of a breaking television news broadcast.

I stepped in because I wanted to see it—this
inbetweenpurgatorywaitingforeverythingtochange
Limbo Room.
I wanted to see
if it contained magic. If it had the power
to indefinitely

Stall—

Stall—

what I knew was coming
for her.
What I know is coming
for all of us.

I wanted to see if Limbo was more—
more than
just a dance where, eventually, everyone
falls down.

Clearly the answer was
no.

Get the Nurse

What can we do for you? they asked.
They were desperate to "do" for me.

So I asked for her.
I asked for her for you.

She was your favorite nurse
so I requested her presence at your death.

She didn't like me
and I didn't like her,

but she was there
to greet you on the day of your arrival

so I invited her to say goodbye
on the day of your departure.

She reminds me of myself at her age,
you once told me over the phone,

but nothing about her reminded me
of you.

Maybe I just didn't know her
well enough.

Or maybe I didn't know you
well enough.

Either way,
they sent for her, and she came

and we stood there, she and I,
like estranged siblings—loving you,

not liking each other.
Not liking each other so much.

At the 55-And-Older Park

There were no sympathy casseroles,
just a fruit salad.
The neighbor knocked, held out a bowl,
and I—grief-gaunt—said
Thank you—didn't have to say
my body is so empty—didn't have to say
I am starving—didn't have to say
where I live, everyone brings food by
after a death
because the neighbor knew
because the neighbor said—
Here—there is too much death—Here
it's hard to keep up with all of the
death—Death
is an expectation because life
has already been over for years.
When death happens,
people will be sad for you
but they're used to death.
And they're on fixed incomes.
So—you may get a sympathy card
(if you're lucky)
but they're going to keep the casseroles
for themselves.

Like a Child

Today a memory hit-slapped-slugged me
and it stung so hard so bad that

like a child
I let out a cry and cursed

that group called "They"
who say, say, and keep saying that

Someday, honey, the memories will make you smile.
Even laugh.

Like a child I trusted.
Like a child I wanted to know how long it would take.

Like a child I asked
Why? Why? Why? Why? Why? Why? Why?

Like a child
I wanted my mom.

They say they are sorry. They say they understand.
They say *just give it more time* and

Bless They Hearts
I know They mean well but

Like a child
I pout, I scream, I shake my fists and say—

Go to Hell!
They can go to Hell.

Without Men

Without men,
she was not sexy.
She was not
a set of boobs or hips.
She was not a barmaid
or waitress
or supper-making
dish-doing, laundry-folding
wife/mother.
Without men,
she was not obliged
to alter her hair,
her face, her molecular structure,
to transform
into a lover. She was not
Pussy Galore.
Without men,
she was not afraid to talk
loud,
laugh loud,
sing,
dance,
live loud.
Without men,
she was not afraid to; of

Flight Violation

She always gave away her oxygen mask.

You take it
she'd say

I'll be fine
she'd say

her inner plane crashing
her body splintered & crushed

her love scattered outward
never inward.

You take it
she'd say

the meat of her—exposed—raw
as hamburger

ir-re-sis-tible
to any self-respecting vulture.

So, I took it.
We all did because

who the hell was going to raise a fist
and stop us?

Sisters

The night nurse and I chatted like long-lost sisters.
Me—
with my chunky glasses, the older one.
She—
with her long, dark ponytail, the younger one.
She—
just beginning her thrust into photography.
Me—
nodding sagely about the obstacles.
Me—
procuring stories of glamorous sounding travel and
You—
sitting in your hospital bed unnoticed, disregarded.
Proud—
to have two daughters instead of only one.
Proud—
that the second daughter has children,
which finally gives you grandchildren.
Proud—
to see me, the first daughter, cooing over the
cheesy, overworked, amateur images embedded
on this second daughter's iPhone.
Proud—
of how I encourage her, how I congratulate her.
Not knowing that—
I honestly don't care about her kids or her pictures.
I'm just bored, and she's just bored and we just want
to talk about ourselves while
You
look on—beaming,
uncomfortably waiting
for us to remember that it's time for your pill.
Proud—
to have two daughters who ignore you
instead of only
one.

Mother/Daughter Day

I pulled my hand out of her hand
somewhere around Maurice's, Cinnabon, or
possibly Orange Julius.

We were having one of our Mother/Daughter days.
They were always at the mall.
Madonna was always singing "Like a Virgin."

It was 1984. I was 14. I was
awkward.

She reached for my hand to reassure me.
To say—I'm always here for you.
To say—Don't grow up just yet.

To say—Don't go
into that dressing room as my only girl, and emerge
as your own woman.

I let go
of her hand.

I let go
of her hand and grabbed a pair of stirrups—
the kind that everyone at school was wearing.

I walked into the dressing room, and
I changed.

Hospital Gossip

Poor woman sat in a hospital bed
alone
after dialysis
in front of food she couldn't eat
without the company of a lover or a friend or
her only child—

poor thing.

Without
her only child, the daughter
she was so proud of, so grateful,
so thankful to have,
who was a thousand miles away, who
came late to the world—late
to her bedside—late
to love, to forgiveness, to maturity—late
to the ICU because that child
was out running again.

She was always running, that girl, always running
to some other place
and by the time she turned around to run back to
this place—that woman—her mother
was gone—

poor thing.

No Father Sister Brother Child

When I decided to kill my mother
the nurse said I was brave.
There was no one to stop me. No one
to consult.

That ragged scar on her belly?
It was my doing. And the drunk doctor's doing.

I bear no belly scars.

At the memorial a friend takes my hand and says;
    When my father died, I was so angry that the world kept turning,
    that people were just out there buying groceries
    and acting like everything was normal when I knew
    that nothing would ever be normal again.

I want to tell her that I am still buying groceries too. Instead
we talk about planting gardens. About yanking weeds
and how good it feels to sink our shaking hands into the earth.

She weeps for her father alongside siblings and children.

We hug. She gives me a look of
understanding. She understands
nothing.

Go away everything, just go away and leave me
to the seeds.

Heir

I'm the only child, the only
heir—so I got

everything.
All of it.

Lucky you, said
an unfriend.

What

could I say.
There was nothing.

My Mother's Boxes

I should go through things,
but I don't.

And then I don't
again and again and again and
now

all of the things in their boxes have been
shoved

into the back of some closet
where spiders have laid claim,
have wrapped

every sealed-up sorrow
in silk.

Look at How I'm Becoming My Mother

Look at how my hair is turning gray
in the same places that hers turned gray.
Look at how my back aches
like her back ached.

Look at my mouth droop
my skin crepe
my neck fold
my arms
wobble. Look—

There she is. Here
we are.

Sterling

There's a wall in my bedroom
where necklaces hang.

Bought and worn by my mother
they are mine now—each one

still clutching a trace of her skin.
Each one—mute.

I never wear them.
Nor the rings or bracelets.

She was always a sucker
for bawdy bling

her delicate hands never without
illumination.

Even at death
she wore silver.

Sour

I thought I could walk
I thought I could walk through
I thought I could walk through the grocery store and put

grapes

apples tomatoes peppers mushrooms cottage cheese
yogurt butter bread chips cans of beans cans of chicken
cans of whatever
into my grocery cart—but
I was already broken
already retreating
by the time I got to the

grapes

because I remembered how
you couldn't eat
how you walked these aisles
alone
in pain
searching
for something—anything
that would settle-in
stay put
digest.

In your freezer I found
Popsicles. They were

grape.

From What I Remember

I was watching a documentary (in my dream)
about a murderer.
There was footage from his childhood
in Wisconsin. There was footage (in my dream)
of his mom,
smiling, bouncing
her baby boy
    that future murderer
    who grew up in my mother's home state
    in my home state
on her knee.
It was the summer of 1950 (in my dream). It was
the twenty-seventh day of June.
The month, date, year
flickered in the lower corner of the TV screen.
When I saw the date
    6/27/1950
I no longer cared (in my dream)
about the innocent baby who grew up to become
the grotesque man.
I didn't move closer to the screen because I wanted to know
what circumstances or chemical imbalances
can turn a baby into a monster.
    I moved closer (in my dream)
because I wanted to see if the sun was shining
on the day that
    my mother
    was born
    6/27/1950

All Along

She was dying all along.
When the doctors said she was
        doing well
they meant,
        for a dying person.
For a person who can no longer
stand or walk or shower on her own,
        she's doing well.

She still has a lot of years in her
said one of the doctors.
The handsome one, the one
all the nurses had a crush on.
        Years,
he said, those Godiva eyes, soothing
that Hyde smile, smug.
        Years,
he said,
two days before
        she died.

Last Man

Afterwards

the first thing he did was text
to say that his preferred funeral home
would be calling me.

Then he texted again

to say that his preferred funeral home
would need my signature to transfer
the body.

Then more texts

about the church, the casket,
and to say that *Your mother would want me
to do the service.*

I should do the service

he shouted, begged, ordered
like some kind of wannabe superhero
who is always too late to the rescue.

He wanted her so badly

when she was alive.
Stand in line
I'd always wanted to say.

I should do the service

he kept telling me with his fingertips
because he wanted her so badly
now that she was dead.

Waiting to Hear

I sent a text message with a picture, and now
I'm waiting to hear back from you.

Meanwhile, I have a
Question—How did you forgive your mother?

Question—How did you know that she was
just a woman—Just a human?

Question—Can you make me more forgiving?
Question—Can you make me less judgmental?

Question—Why did it take your death for me to learn
that you were just a woman—Just a human?

Question—Did you like the picture?
I'm wearing your robe, wrapped in your blanket,

and waiting to hear from you—every day,
I'm waiting to hear.

Grief Semantics

In the distance, I heard someone say
Life goes on.

I wanted to sit them down. I wanted to say
Listen up—

The TV
goes on. The lamp
goes on. The a.m. radio
goes on. The dishwasher
goes on. The answering machine
goes on. The chainsaw, weed whacker, refrigerator,
goes on. The water pump, computer, coffee pot, kitchen light
goes on. Life does not
go on. Life
ends.

Time
goes on.

There's a difference.

Piece of Meat

Is there meat?
your third husband would say.

Sloppy Joes? Kielbasa and kraut? Chicken
and dumplings? Tacos?

There better be meat.

Sometimes there wasn't meat. Sometimes
there was soup

because there wasn't enough money
for meat.

Where's the meat?
your third husband would say, not asking, but

demanding, accusing, faulting.

Wasn't it he? Who owed child support?
Alimony?

Wasn't it you? Paying the bills?
Wasn't it you?

Paying?

1987

Back then the grocery stores were local.
Local families owned them,
stocked the shelves, tallied the totals.
The local clerks knew us
by name and budget—Back then

the local clerks waved to my mother and said,
"Hello one-hundred-dollars-a-week-lady!"

They called her that because her budget was
$100 a week. $100 a week
to feed a husband, a daughter, the husband's two sons,
and herself—Back then
there was a family. For a little while

that family ate a lot of Spam.
And to tell you the truth, we liked it.

Bananas

I went to the store to buy bananas because
I always buy bananas and it felt like
a normal thing to do.

When it was my turn to pay, I set the
cheery yellow bunch—each fruit shaped like a smile
on to the conveyor belt and the clerk said

Hello, how are you today?

I wanted to say,
My mother just died.

I wanted to say,
I don't even know if I can eat these bananas
or anything else
ever again.

I wanted to say,
This is a grocery store not a therapy session,
why must you ask me such an impossible question?

I said,
I think I'm going bananas

which made the clerk look up at me
and laugh.

The Age of Loss

After the one-year mark passes
moms and dads clock the age of their babies
who are no longer babies
by saying their baby is
13 months old.

What about people
who are no longer
people—people
who have turned into ash
and air?

How do we clock—

    the loss

is a newborn—just seconds old
then minutes, hours,
days.

        Loss grows

1-month crying
2-months reaching
loss is growing

    so big!

6-months sitting
9-months walking

1-year talking—No! (*the first word*)
incessantly, eternally repeating itself—

No
No
No
No
No
Please—(*second word*)

No.

Obituary Notes

Loved
sheep, cows, horses, cats, dogs, cranes.

Had
brown hair, blonde hair, silverish-brownish-blonde hair.
Long, long nails. Long, long hair. Short nails. Short hair.
Medium length nails. Medium length hair.

Big laugh. Filled a room with her laugh.

Loved
spinning wheels, knitting needles, yarn.

Had a knack
for taking blurry pictures with poor
composition.

Had
a squinty-eyed smile, blue-ish teeth
colored by old dental fillings, yellow-ish teeth
colored by coffee and cigarettes.

Hated
winter, grocery store lines, mirrors.

Loved
dancing, sunshine, heat, bold color, weak beer,
ham, cheese, soft cookies, white bread.

Loved. Loved. Loved. Loved. Loved
the wrong men.

Had a knack.

Character Study

The way I once played

Scrooge—my voice rearranged.
Venom and spittle clouding
the air.

How the audience held its breath.
The way they stood and clapped as I
bowed.

How I sent my mother a picture
of my unrecognizable face. The way it looked
like white tissue

ripped
from the safety of its box—used, crumpled,
tossed.

The way it looked
like her face

when a drunk doctor ripped me out
of her red gut—and later
when a gentle nurse zipped
the white bag
shut.

How I held my breath.

Chimera

My mother sat
    across the table
wearing the sweater that I am wearing
    now.

Where are you? I asked.
    She didn't answer.

Where are you? I asked again,
and all those years—where
was I, was I, was I?
    She didn't answer.

She was
    a movie scene
    a motion picture, chewing
    a peanut butter cookie, scrunching
    her shoulders with
delight. I was
    a movie-goer, an audience member
riveted, my voice—

ech-ech-echoing.

At the Grad Party

I remember how she stood, frowning
behind the butcher block.
The knife was sharp, but the cheddar
was crumbling. And the marriage
was crumbling.

The cheddar went first,
but maybe it was foreshadowing,
and maybe she saw the shadow
in the crumbles,
which would explain why she drove the knife
so fiercely
into the flesh
of the waxy orange rectangle
and yelled at, and blamed
the waxy orange rectangle for
every-single-thing-that-had-ever-gone-wrong
in her life.

It's just cheese, Mom, I said,
then stole a piece and popped it into my mouth
as if to prove that everything was okay, that there was
no reason for her to crumble—no reason
for her to melt.

Two Daughters One Mother

I watched as they posed for a photo—arms
around each other's shoulders—heads
bent, touching—hair
woven together by wind,
the older one's silver strands
catching the sun.

Both are daughters, only one
is a mother. The mother
is always worrying because
the daughter is always

disappearing.

But today
they are together. Today
they are posing for a photo
the way we used to.

Versions of each other
they are
holding hands—the daughter
loose fingered, fidgety.
The mother—gripping,
holding on

so tight.

Conspiracy

After Lucille Clifton

Someone was always conspiring to kill you.
Your father, sister,
1st husband, 3rd husband,
me
the baby so stubborn inside you—you
pushing pushing pushing. Or possibly
me
pushing pushing pushing and
you
clutching the bed rails, holding on,
already not ready to let go—already
begging for a little more
than I could give you—you
conspiring to kill
you.

A Courteous Girl

There are Christmas cards to write
to people I don't love

but I'll do it

because it would have made my mother
happy

happy to know she'd raised a courteous girl
a girl who apologizes

for her shortcomings
by writing Christmas cards to the living

shivering

as she writes
as if Ol' Frosty himself were in the room

as if she might be able to save
Ol' Frosty

might be able to stop his meltdown
and hers

by stuffing envelopes
full of bullshit *Season's Greetings.*

At the Public Library

It must have been a terrible shock when
I ran into him at the public library and he said
Hello—Nice day—How's your mother?

A terrible shock when I, skinny with grief,
whispered to him that
she was dead.

Years ago, he bought a car from her.

That day,
at the public library, his face turned pink
and he took a step back.

He wasn't afraid of me. He was afraid
of the way his tongue was twisting, thickening,
choking his words.

I'm sorry, I said. I said
the words for him. I said the words
for her.

What Set Me Off Crying

It was that onion.
Not the raw one;
the fried one—
so richly caramelized
so onion-ring-y
so infused with
the image of you
sitting across from me
both of us indulging
in those breaded
forbidden
ketchup-smothered
rings—
a group of obnoxious
20-somethings
loudly impressing
no one
in the background.
We couldn't hear
ourselves speak
but we didn't need to
speak—
we were chewing.
Our tongues
were mashing.
Our eyes
were giggling.
Our eyes were saying—
we're going to regret this,
we're *never*
going to regret this.

Barstool

My mother fell off the barstool.
Someone pulled her by the hair, and she landed
on her head.

Men looked on
annoyed
that her body blocked their beer path.

She didn't move.

From the corner, I watched.
Her waist-long hair was splayed across a floor
dirtied by shoe prints and spilled gin.

Her thick, tight thighs lay limp. Heeled shoes
lightly clung to her motionless feet—
half on, half off.

My grandfather peered over the bar—his bar
where his daughter lay outstretched
on the floor.

Duty-bound,
he followed his diseased stomach
past the cash register

and through the saloon-style swing-door
to take a look.
With a foot on either side of her crooked hips

my grandfather bent and held his knees.
He squinted
and checked for breath.

One decent moment
before he tossed, by wrist & ankle,
his daughter, my mother,

on to the empty pool table like a tied-up calf.
I wailed—but by then
the jukebox was playing again.

BS Happy Endings

I'm reading "One of the Best Books of the Year."
Years ago, it won the Pulitzer.
The copy in my hands is
a used paperback with a corner fold on page 285.
I do not fold corners.
Someone else, some reader-turned-vandal,
folded the corner.

I find myself smoothing the crease made by the vandal.
I find myself thinking of you—of *me* scolding *you*
because *you* were a corner folder.
But I only scold you in my head because
#1—You are dead
#2—I am a snob who thought the books you read weren't "important."
Who thought those books probably deserved to be vandalized because
they were just throw-away, mass-market thrillers filled with
rugged men, unrealistic romances, and BS happy endings.

In other words,
everything-you-ever-wanted-in-life-but-never-got.

You liked to fold once, then twice,
pressing your thumbnail hard
on the creases—an experienced editor
adding in all of the wounds and scars that the author
cut.

But who folds the pages of a Pulitzer?
What could possibly be missing
from a Pulitzer?

That's when I hear you laughing, scolding me back, saying,
Sweet child, here's what's missing—
Rugged men, unrealistic romances, and BS happy endings.

After You Left

So this is how it feels to be alone.

I think I'd rather not be.

But thanks for dropping by
and entering my life
and becoming my friend
and doing my dishes
and recalling my memories
and sharing yours
and teaching me more patience
and sharing your onion rings
and laughing and questioning
and sharing your clothes
and exploring the world
and sharing your wine
and tying my shoes
and sharing your coffee
and taking photographs
and sharing your honey
and buying me cheese
and walking through parks
and holding my hand
and driving to beaches
and singing off-key
and altogether loving me
and leaving me behind.

Empathy Has an Ego

She's always with you
people say, and
when people first started saying it
I wanted to slap people's faces
because I hated
those pitiful smiles
        until I realized
people did not pity me, people
were only thinking
        as they looked at me
about themselves
about their own pain
about how
        in their own after-death lives
their faces looked like my face
about how
my ache
was a mirror, a reflection, a reminder
of their ache
about how much
they wanted me
        or maybe needed me
to believe them when they said
        She's always with you
so they could go home, bury their faces
into an old sweater and believe it
when they whispered the words
        You are always with me
over and over
into empty arms of yarn—nevermind
the stale smell—nevermind
the moths.

Revision Notes

Once upon a time there was a girl.
    (*This is a good start*)

But *don't* say she grew up in a home where
she had to call the police because her father
was choking her mother.
And *don't* say she married three times.
Or divorced three times.
Or that she nearly died in childbirth at the age of 19.

Say she married *once* and that her husband
never hit, cheated, lied or drank.

She had a big laugh.
    (*This part requires no revision*)

But take away the cancer and pneumonia
and especially the chapter about how
the daughter leaves the hospital on Monday, says
See you on Thursday!
and then the mom dies on Wednesday.
    (*Too sad*)

Have it go something like—

Daughter picks mom up on Thursday—as planned.
They go home—as planned.
They snack on cheese and crackers.
They talk and laugh, and when
they turn on the TV, they discover that there is finally
    World Peace!

And that Elvis
    isn't dead!
All this time Elvis has been
    Alive!
And get this—He's been living right next door to
    Mom!
Mom and Elvis fall in love and live happily ever after.
    The End.

(Remember, Mom is the main character.
Mom shouldn't die. Revise the story.)

I Say

You don't call or text and neither do I.
We don't speak, but

I talk to you every day.
I say—hello.

I say—I am driving your car.
I am wearing your clothes.

I say—your life was such a series of house fires
but your body is such a small pile of ashes.

I say—I'm sorry.

I say—as if writing a postcard from across the world—
Wish you were here.

We Go On

The plates and cups go here, the forks go there.
The pans, the coffee pot, the wine glasses go
here, there, and there.

How do we do it? How do we go on? After the final
phone call, kiss, hug, LOL, I love you. How
do we go on?

How do we *not* go on?

How do we go on? How do we *not* go on?
How do we go on? How, how, how, how,
how?

The plates and cups go here, the forks go there.
We go on, we go on, we go on, on, on, on
here, there, and there
we go, go, go, go
on.

Sunshine State

The price to fly to Fort Myers
has gone down.

You're not there, but
I could still buy a ticket. I could
pretend. I could
fly into the sun, into
that merciful, blinding light
where the reality of your absence
might be obscured, momentarily
stifled by
the amnesiac heat
the sweet stupor of margaritas
the mad excitement of seeing all those bikinis
& hearing all those Elvis impersonators
& spying all those dolphins
& finding all those sand dollars.

The price of delusion has gone down, but oh—
Oh, what I would pay.

Frequently Asked Questions

What happened?
How did what happened, happen?
Where are you?

Are you happy?
Are you free from worry?
And pain?

Have you forgiven yourself, your father, your sister
your 1st & 2nd & 3rd husbands?
What about me?

Can you ever forgive me?

What did they do wrong?
What did I do wrong? What did I do
right?

What do I do with your clothes, jewelry, yarn, scarves,
scarves (so many scarves), your car, house, furniture,
cat?

Who should I blame?
What do I do with my pocked memories?
How do I fill in the blanks?

I still have questions.
Why didn't I ask more questions?
What happened? What did they do wrong?

Who should I blame?

Why do your ashes, when I toss them into
sunlight, moonlight, water or air, always look like smoke
and glitter?

Ephemeral

There's an oversized magnet on my refrigerator.
It's an image of flowers with fern-like leaves,
each bloom a layered spectrum of tangerine.

I don't recognize the flowers, but I like
how they hang there—preserved forever
in a cellophane sarcophagus.

Maybe, like you, they've gone extinct. Maybe
the image is just a beautiful rendition
of the past

like all of those yellowed photographs that are
glued to the pages of "The Good Old Days"
photo albums that my older self opens

when I want to revisit my younger self—
that thick, honeyed girl who didn't
know   anything.

Tough Love

I know you are gone
but lately

I feel like you are still here—
living in me, taking over me.

It's time. Time
for you to leave. Pack up.

Go—on your next adventure.

Remember how you pushed me
out the door toward seventh grade?

How I begged to stay?
How you said,

Go—I cannot shelter you.

Oh, you confessed years later, *Oh,*
how I cried for you then.

It's my turn now. My turn
to push. My turn

to release my daughterhood
from your motherhood, to say,

Go—I cannot shelter you.

Oh, how I cry—how I almighty wail
for you now.

Sometimes It Was Like This

Everyone loves Michelle
    said my husband.

Yeah, I don't know why
    said my mother.

She wasn't always nice
    to me.

I wasn't always nice
    to her.

Through the Cracks

The pen that I intended to use to write a poem
about my mother
fell through the cracks.

Do you see how the words
"My mother fell through the cracks"
could stand alone?

I could have started the poem this way, but
it was the pen that tumbled, fell
through the cracks of a deck—the pen
that led me to think of how my mother tumbled, fell
through the cracks of deck after deck after deck
and how maybe your mother
(or father, sister, brother, child)
fell too.

I'll never be able to reach that pen. It's gone
for good—or bad
all of the life inside of it stuck in some dark place
because of a cliché twist of fate or gust
of wind or foolish negligence or
all of the above.

And really, does it matter
how
it happened or
why or when?
It happened and that's that.

Get a new pen, I tell myself.
It's the least you can do.

It's the only thing I can do.

ICU

I keep thinking of the way

her eyebrows lifted and her forehead wrinkled
when she heard me say

Hi.

As if she'd been
                              stranded

in a dream
and in the dream she was

                              stranded

on some undiscovered island

and suddenly—there I was
driving a rescue boat—there I was

unable to save her.

What I Know

I know how to push pain
dulling fluids into closed mouths.

I know how to hold a cold hand, kiss
a cold face, sing songs, recite poems, tell stories
to closed eyes, open mouths.

I know how to cry-laugh or laugh-cry
depending on which of those two
maniacal emotions declares itself
the alpha, depending on
the memory, depending on
the time of day or night or wee hour
in between
day and night, in between
life and death, depending on
which maniacal emotion
seizes my throat.

I know how to sit
at the side of a bed and read quietly
to myself. I know how
to let the body occupying that bed
breathe deep, then shallow   then
not at all.

I know how.

Hurricane

There were no direct flights.
You didn't trust your car.
I had to coordinate a ride.
Uber was too expensive and

There was a Hurricane.

I had a show.
I had rehearsals before the show.
I had to harvest chard, tomatoes,
summer squash and beets.
I had to work as long as I could to stay
as long as I could and

There was a Hurricane.

The nurses thought you were fine.
The doctors thought you were fine.
The O.T. and the P.T. thought you were fine.
I arrived on Friday, left on Monday,
blew you a kiss and said
See you on Thursday!

You died on Wednesday.
It was sunny
and warm
and

There was a Hurricane.

Florida State Statute

If you have no spouse—
      Florida is allowed to kill you.
If your children are over the age of 25—
      Florida is allowed to kill you.
No spouse + No young children =
      No such thing as wrongful death.
      No such thing as malpractice.
No spouse + No young children =
      A Florida State Statute that says
      Florida is allowed to kill you.

Florida is allowed to kill you,
eat a sandwich,
drink a coffee and
forget about you
until a more convenient time such as
a dinner party
where everyone is drunk
and confessing their legal sins during a game of
Truth or Dare that turns into
Truth
that turns into
Guilt
that turns into
Absolution
that transforms into a martini-flavored anthem
of thanks and praise in honor of—

Florida,
     The Sunshine State
Florida,
     Where the Sawgrass Meets the Sky
Florida,
     In God We Trust
     the divine state statute that says
Florida
     is allowed to kill you.

The Experience of Lying Near Death

Lying there
I let go of judgment.

And anger.
And labels.
And
Right versus Wrong.
And
You versus Me.

Lying there
I let go of ego.
I let go of excuses.

Lying there
I told the truth
and I didn't care
who heard me.

Making Future Plans

As if it were an option
I begin to imagine myself
standing in my mother's kitchen.

I have just returned from a run.
I am making tea. She is making coffee.
I spoon out honey, cream, and then
we both sit—pass another hour—just talking.
About what, I don't know. It doesn't matter.

A neighbor knocks on the door to tell us something
insignificant. We observe
the cat running through the house—a sure sign
that he has just pooped. We cheer him on,
laughing.

A pair of cranes walk past the pond,
gurgling. They are so elegant and awkward.

We plan our day. It's simple.
Eat. Walk. Savor

the sun, the heat,
the fact of our togetherness,
of our exclusive, uninterrupted time
which (like Christmas) only happens
once a year.

Pull a chair up to the ocean. Marvel
at the breeze
as if it will not be our last breeze. Marvel
at the day
as if it will not be
our last day.

Take a selfie. Marvel
at our big, toothy, ignorant grins.

I Can't Believe

that your cat is purring
in someone else's lap

that your closets are holding
someone else's clothes

that your clothes are covering
someone else's body

that your body holds
no form

that your body casts
no shadow

that your body could be mistaken
for a pile of cigarette ash

and swept away by a breeze
or a broom.

As a Consequence of Loss

All of the birthday & Christmas & Easter cards
have stopped.

All of the letters
written in a flowery hand with big circles hovering
above the lowercase "i's"
have stopped.

All voice messages
that reliably began with the words, *Well, hi honey*
have stopped.

All text messaging has stopped.

All package deliveries, each box
taped so tight that I always needed a knife
to cut them open
have stopped.

All jokes about the taped packages
have stopped.

Oh, how we'd laugh about those packages.
That damn tape.
The extra ounces it added.
The extra shipping cost it added.
The extra struggle it added when I held the phone
between my ear and shoulder so I could use both hands
to pry the parcel open.

Oh,
how I'd groan & grit my teeth.
Oh,
how we'd laugh and laugh.

All laughter has stopped.

The Tea Room

Inside,
a haughty host is dressed
in a top hat and a suit with
two tails. The waitresses wear
colorful tiaras & matching bowties.

It's all meant to be romantic. It's all meant
to take us back in time, to help us
          pretend
as we eat our quiche (a house favorite)
followed up by
bread pudding (another house favorite)
          that the past is still the present
which would mean that—

Any minute now
          my mother will walk
          out of the Ladies Room
          and back to our table where
          she'll sit down
          right next to me, smile,
          touch my hand,
          and take a sip of water.
Any minute now.

After Life

there's the sadness
the thinking about
all the faceless people around me
who are still alive
wondering why
they are still alive why
you are not
wondering
how does blood flow cease
how does water flow continue
why do we say "rock solid"
when referring to breakable things
like a rock
in the shape of a heart
that is lying on a beach
split in half

Still Rabid

I congratulate myself
because I haven't cried
in weeks.

I think—
Maybe I'm progressing.
Maybe

I'm moving out
of grief into
healing.

And then a random memory
rips me apart
as I brush my teeth and

my face contorts, my lungs
heave,
my hands shake, my toothbrush

drips
and my mouth—my mouth
foams.

Glutton

Hey, you out there.
You
who have lost someone
to whatever comes next after whatever
this is. Hey—
You.

Do you ever find yourself
sitting peacefully only to be torpedoed
by an unasked-for memory that sends your eyes to work
blinking and blinking, your mouth to work
quivering, your tongue to work
absorbing the salty sting of the tear that rolls in
through the crack of your lips
like warm rain?

Damn that's painful
and inconvenient
and stuffed
with love—a love that glistens
like a Thanksgiving turkey—the kind
that you want to sink your teeth into—the kind
that lures you in for second and third helpings
and even though you know it might make you sick
you keep going back for more and more again
because it feels so good to feel—it feels so good
to ache your way through the flash
of how that gone person used to push
and goad, and wink, and say—
Have some more. Come on, just a little bit
more, more, more, more,
more.

Now That She's Gone

If I decide to sell my house
no one will try to stop me. No one

will point out the ways in which regret
might grip me

or how the flowers, without my hands to tend them,
might wilt, die, or never bloom at all.

When I sleep at a rest area in the back of my car
or bicycle through France

carrying all of my food, all of my water
and a tent

no one will call or text. No one
will worry.

If I steal, cheat, lie, pillage, murder,
or do damn well all of it

under the high command of God
or whiskey

no one
will forgive me.

Pieces

Someone asked if I had kept a piece
of my mother's clothing.

A piece? I thought as I stood there wearing her bra.
And her shorts. And her shirt.

They are all too big for me,
but I don't care.

I wear her
robe, pajamas, socks, hair ties, hand-knit scarves—

A piece?

I have a wardrobe.

Is that weird?

Is it weird to wrap my body inside the limp fabrics
that once absorbed my mother's perfumes

and suck in the last
of her scent?

Her blood is my blood. Her body
is my body. When I sweat

beneath her bra, her shirt, her shorts—
I'm not quite as lonely and

she's not quite as dead.

Sacred God

"Sacré Dieu," is an old French curse meaning "sacred God."
More pious, and more acceptable, is "sacré bleu" because bleu
(blue) rhymes with Dieu (God) and avoids taking God's
name in vain.

Sacré bleu!

my mother "cursed" when I was 9
and she was 29 and the toaster blew up.

Sacré bleu!

my mother "cursed" when I was 29
and she was 49 and I moved far away.

Sacré Dieu!

I cursed, for real, when I was 49
and my mother was 69

and she was lying in a bed,
dying, and I was

farewell kissing her
sacré face.

Sacré Dieu!

I cursed—*Oh, Sacred God,*
damn you.

In Repose

I see you
in someone else's eyes
in someone else's clothes
in the leaves of a palm tree
in a poem I didn't write
in the butterfly I think I saw but am not quite sure I saw
in January—
in the movies
in my dreams, though never often enough—
in my own eyes
in my own aging face
in the white strands of my own turning-white hair
in my own hip and hand gestures
in yarn that you spun that I wrap and unwrap
in order to entertain the cat
in the morning—
in someone else's laugh
in a country song
in a country home magazine
in sloppy joes
in two-for-one margaritas
in joy, though never often enough—
in rage, too often
in fear, too often
in love, too often
in pain, too long—alone
in a room too long
in repose
in breathless
repose

The Trouble with Being a Childless Only Child

Who will remember you when I am no longer here
to remember you? Who
will remember your hands?
Those sleek fingers made to hold, to so artfully display
an array of turquoise rings? Or your laugh—
the way you bent over, held your belly and
cried out? And how
the dental fillings that made your molars turn blue
had a neon glow?

When I'm gone no one will ever know
that I stood here, at what is now my kitchen sink,
writing, worrying
over this newly discovered form of loss.
No one will ever know

that before this discovery I was preparing
to make pear sauce
out of pears that I picked from my neighbor's tree
while listening to an interview with the artist
Dario Robleto who believes that
love survives the death of cells

which would mean we're good for now because
your hands, your glowing blue molars, your laugh, your cells
are here
in my cells, and I'm alive, and
I love you—but

who will remember
your hands, your glowing blue molars, your laugh, your cells
when I am not alive, when I am not here
to remember you?

And who will pick those luscious pears?

Shared

Her body
with man.

Her body
with child.

Reincarnation Prayer for My Mother

Go. Leave. Come back. Come back
to a place like Ireland this time.

Find a good man—just *one* this time.
Get married—just *once* this time.

Have babies, *more than one* this time.
Redheads this time.

Raise sheep. Spin wool. Weave. Knit. Craft
a good life, a family life this time.

Go. Leave. Don't come back here. Stay
away from here this time.

Be happy this time.

ACKNOWLEDGMENTS

Thank you to the editors of the following publications in which some of these poems first appeared:

"It Takes You by Surprise," *After the Pause*
"Making Future Plans," *Autumn Sky Poetry Daily*
"Hospital Gossip," "Bananas," *Tabula Rasa Review*
"WWJD," *Welter Online*
"Mother/Daughter Day," *Writing in a Woman's Voice*

Thank you to Dr. Ross Tangedal and the devoted team of UW-Stevens Point students and staff at Cornerstone Press for taking such care in the publication of this book. My mother would be astonished—there is no greater gift.
My love and thanks to all *The Book of She* "Sheros" who brought joy back into my life. Your enthusiasm and encouragement enabled me to wade into the raw grief that was essential to the truth telling of these poems. Special thanks to Pat Carlson for being a willing and generous editor, Mark Reis, best friend and devoted cat dad, and to my dearest poetry buddy, Jacqueline West, for invaluable feedback delivered so tenderly.
And finally, thanks to my husband, Robert, my truest friend, deepest love, and the one person who listened to every word of every poem, often more than once—often more than twice. Everybody loves you, but I love you most.

MICHELLE MEYER is the author of *The Book of She* (2021). Her poems have appeared in *Under Her Eye: A Blackspot Books Anthology, Autumn Sky Poetry Daily, Nebulous, Remington Review, Tabula Rasa Review, Welter Online,* and *Zoetic,* among others. In addition, Michelle is a worldwide house and pet sitter who especially loves cats. She lives in Western Wisconsin.

www.ingramcontent.com/pod-product-compliance
Lightning Source LLC
Chambersburg PA
CBHW031443120626
46545CB00006B/2529